The
BOOK *of* LOVE
and
FORGIVENESS

MICHAEL MIRDAD

GRAIL
PRESS

The Book of
Love and Forgiveness

GRAIL
PRESS

PO Box 1908
Sedona, AZ 86339
(360) 671-8349
www.MichaelMirdad.com

Book cover and interior design by
Robert Lanphear
www.lanpheardesign.com

Library of Congress Cataloging-in-Publication Data
Mirdad, Michael.
The Book of Love and Forgiveness/ Michael Mirdad.
Library of Congress
ISBN: 978-0-9855079-7-8

ACKNOWLEDGEMENTS

I first want to thank anyone who has ever supported my work, which includes those who are currently sponsors or supporters.

My heartfelt thanks go to Lynne Matous for her superb editing and to David Brown, Gregg Matous, Judy Messer, Joy Nanda, Joan Belle Nemeth, and Linda Mae Costello for their great proofreading and invaluable feedback. Also, thanks to Bob Lanphear for his continued brilliant book and cover design, as well as Christian Kurz for the inception of this cover design.

Last, but not least, I give thanks to the Divine Mother—the Voice of God—that calls us all to the lesson of forgiveness.

CONTENTS

PREFACE

This is not just a book *about* love and forgiveness. It certainly clarifies these topics, but more importantly, it takes us *through* the process of loving and forgiving. So instead of reading *about* love and forgiveness and their profound effects, you, the reader, will come to understand and experience what love and forgiveness truly are and are not. You will come to know that **love is who we are, and that forgiveness is what love does**—at least until forgiveness is no longer necessary. In effect, you will become far more the embodiment of love and forgiveness—which is our most important purpose on earth.

After reading this book, the "act" of forgiveness will be much easier. It will be easier because you will have learned about, and accepted, your identity as love at a deeper level, and because **you will have gone through the process of integrating forgiveness into your consciousness—possibly without even realizing it**.

One of the most beautiful things about love and forgiveness, however, is that love and forgiveness are neither *human* nor *humane* acts, as most people might think. Instead, **love is a reflection of Divine Consciousness, and forgiveness is the natural act that comes from that Consciousness.** Therefore, forgiveness is love in action—originating from deep within our heart and soul, where true love is found. It's an action that we can only choose, share, and experience *after* we have accessed the deepest part of our heart and soul.

This does not mean, however, that we have to be "religious" or even "spiritual" to practice forgiveness. But we do have to *access*, or remember, love. Also, **we must be willing (even if just a little) to see someone or something in a new and different light**.

Eventually, **after witnessing the profoundly positive effects of love and forgiveness in one area of our life, it becomes irresistible to practice forgiveness in *every* other area.** Then, the day will come when we will choose to forgive (release) every judgmental perception we have ever had on every person or event. We can then choose to release all limited beliefs and judgmental perceptions of everything. **This process first helps us to become better people. Then it leads us into a complete remembrance of our divinity.**

Introduction to Love and Forgiveness

The most important subject on earth a person can study is spirituality. Love is the most important topic related to spirituality. And **the greatest manifestation or expression of love is that of forgiveness.**

There is no love without forgiveness,
and there is no forgiveness without love.

–Bryant H. McGill

Consequently, although most people have a very limited or misdirected understanding of forgiveness, it is the most important gift and expression of love that we can offer to ourselves and/ or to others.

We could accurately say that **forgiveness is the very foundation of life, because** *without* **forgiveness, we are never truly alive. Holding onto past wounds and judgments makes us part of the "walking dead."**

To err is human; to forgive, divine.

–Alexander Pope

Forgiveness is neither real nor truly effective when it isn't inspired by love or when it is offered out of duty or obligation.

To say "I am going to forgive so and so because it's something I have to do" will not lead to a positive outcome—at least not one that will be deep or long-lasting.

The truth is that if people tell us they are going to forgive us for something because they feel obliged to do so, we probably should refuse the offer. It's not that we shouldn't appreciate the seemingly good intentions, but we might ask them if, instead, they would be willing to go through an *authentic* process of forgiveness. Even though all forms of forgiveness are helpful to some extent; **when we experience the higher forms, or expressions, of love-based forgiveness, it's unlikely we will ever again settle for anything less.**

This is one of the many reasons that forgiveness is more like a process than a one-time event. Our initial response towards someone who seems to have harmed us is usually a feeling of hurt, which often shifts to either anger or sadness or sometimes even numbness. But as we progress through the stages of forgiveness, we eventually will feel neutral—which most people often confuse for completion in their healing process—but it is not. There is still one stage remaining. If we practice authentic forgiveness, it will eventually result in feeling peace—a "peace that surpasses understanding." In other words, where we once experienced either negative feelings or no feelings at all, we will know—with greater certainty—that we have completely forgiven someone, not when we feel neutral or feel nothing, but when we feel peaceful whenever we think of that person. Of course, if the harms have felt horrendous, our feeling peace may seem an unlikely possibility. However, what is impossible for us is possible for God.

This book takes us in a full circle, beginning and ending with Love. First, it reveals the relationship between love, judgment, and forgiveness. Understanding and experiencing true forgiveness leads us to greater depths of love, from which we remember that *Love* is what we are created to be. When we forget this truth, we *judge* ourselves and others. Authentic forgiveness releases this judgement and restores us to the truth of who we are—which is love.

Love and Forgiveness are all that really matter. Love is who we are and Forgiveness is what we need to practice when we forget who we are. Again, we are Love, but it's important to forgive ourselves whenever we forget that we are Love.

> *Forgiveness does not exonerate the perpetrator. Forgiveness liberates the victim. It's a gift you give yourself.*

> −T. D. Jakes

Forgiveness is a gift we give to ourselves and to all other people in the world, as we choose to see Divine Love within all beings. And it's important to forgive ourselves whenever we fail to see that Love. Even when the behaviors of other people tempt us to see something besides Love, it is our job and our destiny to shift back to seeing only the Love. This might sometimes seem impossible; but again, what seems impossible for mankind is possible for the divine within mankind. Besides, choosing to see Love is the only way to create "Heaven on earth."

The ascension of our planet, and our race, will not come by way of the correct diet, chanting, meditations, or other such practices, although they are certainly part of the recipe. Forgiveness alone is the essential ingredient for our ascension.

THE ROLE OF CHRIST

Some people have issues with the name "Christ," arising from the atrocities committed by the Christian religion. However, "Christ" is actually not a name, but a title. Therefore, it's helpful if we understand that the historic man named **Jesus, and the consciousness he attained, known as Christ, have nothing directly to do with the religion known as "Christianity."** Therefore, it might help us forgive Jesus, and ourselves for projecting our issues onto him, if we would separate the man Jesus from those who hypocritically use the name "Christ." If that doesn't work, let's forgive the man Jesus for all the harm the church has done in his name.

The word "Christ" is best translated as "the name of the Presence of God within mankind." **The name "Jesus Christ" then simply translates as "Jesus who remembered he is the Christ and is One with God."** This title awaits us all, with our own name being added before the word "Christ." This is one meaning of the line in the Book of Revelation that tells us the "Second Coming of Christ" involves our being "given a new name."

So, by accepting the name "Christ" and what it represents, we are accepting our own divinity. Then, at some point, we also will recognize that this Christ (or divinity) we accept as existent within *us* is also in everyone else—albeit not always obvious. As we learn to accept this—or at least the possibility of it—**it becomes easier to forgive others and ourselves because we realize that everyone is the Christ, waiting to be remembered**. However, if we allow the flaws of others to stand in our way of beholding this Holy Presence within our fellow brothers and sisters, the Presence of Christ within us will remain invisible as well.

Perceiving this Holiness in ourselves and others is dependent upon our ability to truly forgive—forgive what others seem to have done and forgive ourselves for allowing this to taint our vision. And, given that Jesus has already accomplished this level of forgiveness for himself, he becomes a perfect guide for us—especially because he knows we are one with him, which allows his Holy Vision to become ours. That's why the scriptures ask us to "let the Christ that was born in Jesus be born in us as well." Therefore, **as we welcome Jesus into our lives as our Teacher and the Master of Masters, the practice of forgiveness becomes much easier. It's easier now because in Christ, forgiveness is already accomplished**. In part, that's what Jesus meant when he spoke his last words before surrendering his spirit. By saying, "It is accomplished," he was affirming that the Christ within him had returned to its Divine and true Identity by accomplishing the forgiveness of the world. And what he did for himself, he did for us all. All we need do now is merely accept it.

> *The Bible says, "Ask in the Name of Jesus Christ"...*
> *A name does not heal, nor does an invocation call forth*
> *any special power. What does it mean then to call on*
> *Jesus Christ?...We have repeatedly said that one who*
> *has perfectly accepted the Atonement for himself can heal*
> *the world. Indeed, he* [Jesus] *has already done so. He has*
> *recognized himself as God created him* [as the Christ],
> *and in so doing he has recognized all living things as part*
> *of him. There is now no limit on his power, because it is the*
> *Power of God. So has his name become the Name of God,*
> *for he no longer sees himself as separate from God... What*

does this mean for you? It means that in remembering Jesus you are remembering God . . . The Name of Jesus Christ as such, is but a symbol. But it stands for love that is not of this world . . . Remembering the Name of Jesus Christ is to give thanks for all the gifts that God has given you . . . Are other teachers possible, to lead the way to those who speak in different tongues? Certainly there are. Would God leave anyone without a very present help in time of trouble; a savior who can symbolize Himself? Yet do we need a many-faceted curriculum, not because of content differences, but because [the form of the teaching] *must shift and change to suit the need. Jesus has come to answer yours.*
In him you find God's Answer.

—A Course in Miracles

PART I

What is
Love?

CHAPTER 1

What is Love?

There has never been a shortage of writers, poets, songwriters, or philosophers who write or talk about love, doing their best to traverse the depths of its meaning. Although their descriptions and definitions might now and then find a place in our heart, the truth is, **no mortal mind is capable of truly understanding the concept of "Love Divine."** This is why *A Course in Miracles* says that "Love . . . is beyond what can be taught."

One reason human beings fall short of grasping the true meaning of love is that **to *know* love, they have to *be* love. And, having forgotten that they *are* love, most human beings have forgotten *how* to be love**—although not from a lack of hoping, wishing, or trying. What has happened is that all human beings once had a complete awareness of love—its truest meaning and fullest expression. However, over many lifetimes, each time they allowed even the slightest judgmental thought, a small portion of their awareness of love disappeared and was replaced by fear and guilt. Eventually, a greater accumulation of judgment (and its accompanying fear) resulted in a lesser amount of love. This process went on until the average human being eventually experienced more fear than love.

Accumulating like toxic waste, judgment and fear poisoned our minds so thoroughly, there seemed to be little chance of

us ever again cleaning-up our mental environment, which left us with a longing for love—a longing beyond anything else we could ever imagine. This longing is what leads us, like the philosopher, to ask ourselves, "what is love?"

Love, in its purest sense, is who and what we are. And when we are being (or experiencing) our true selves, we think, feel, and act lovingly.

> *Teach* [Think, feel, believe, and demonstrate] *only love,*
> *for that is what you are.*
>
> —*A Course in Miracles*

We are love because God is Love and we are made in God's Image. And since God is eternal, Love is eternal. This also means that **we are eternally the *presence* of love.** And just as a church is built around a sacred altar wherein we perform a ceremony to God, so too is there a church built around the altar of love within our heart and soul. It is here, at this altar, that we find love and discover God.

When we forget that we are love, we begin to judge ourselves—which then leads to judging others. Judging others then leads to the manifestation of unloving experiences. But **if we forgive and release our judgments of self and others, we return to love—which results in the manifestation of loving experiences.**

The remembering of love cannot be realized without the assistance of God—specifically the Mother aspect of God—commonly referred to as the Holy Spirit. Although it is the Divinely Blissful, *Father* aspect of God that created us, it is the Divinely Loving, *Mother* aspect of God that calls us to remember the Truth of our being.

The Holy Spirit, or Divine Mother, is the result of God extending Itself as Love in order to save Its Holy Children. When we, the Children of God, seemingly descended into the universe, the Divine Mother became the Universal Womb in which to catch us when we fell. In so doing, it remains certain that, even in the illusion of a world outside of Heaven, we can never be removed from God.

Again, love is who and what we truly are. But **True Love has very little or nothing to do with what humans perceive as love**. Love has nothing to do with romantic feelings, which come and go, nor does it have anything to do with the particular, special people, things, and events in our life that we claim to love.

> *Only by Love can men see me, and know me,*
> *and come to me.*
>
> *—Bhagavad Gita*

True Love has nothing to do with ever-changing paradigms, conditions, or opinions, because it is changeless. Instead, **True Love is Divine Love, and Divine Love is unconditional and lasts forever**.

An act, or extension, of True Love, for example, sees the light of God in all others even when they cannot see it for themselves.

Love between human beings is typically perceived as something that is passive, weak, and vulnerable, or susceptible to change and attack. Quite the contrary, **True Love is actually active, strong, and free from, or impervious to, any form of attack whatsoever**.

True Love and those who love truly are impervious to harm and attack, not because love is a force stronger than all forms of attack, but because **in reality, there is only love and therefore, love has no opposite.** When human beings come to realize this, their perception of love will no longer be one of weakness.

The opposite of love is fear,
but what is all-encompassing can have no opposite.

—*A Course in Miracles*

Love loves Love. And since God is Love, this means God loves Love and God loves God. So **when we hear that we should love all people and things, all that is really required of us is to Love the Love within them (not the hurtful part of them) because only the Love is real.** This does not, however, mean that we are to love nor hate the *hate* we see in ourselves or others. Since hate is not of God, it is not real. And since it is not real, there is nothing to love nor hate. We can, however, love the hell out of hate until we see only the Love that remains. Also, **we don't have to love harmful events but we can love whatever it is we might learn *from* those events.**

Love does not [really] *"conquer" all things,*
but it does set all things right.

—*A Course in Miracles*

It is helpful to practice recognizing expressions or manifestations of love, and then showing our appreciation by loving these expressions. This includes loving people who love who they truly are (beyond the ego) and whatever they do that is in alignment with their spiritual purpose. We can choose to love and appreciate all forms of goodness, including vulnerability, authenticity, and integrity.

*There are two basic motivating forces: fear and love. When we
are afraid, we pull back from life. When we are in love, we
open to all that life has to offer with passion, excitement, and
acceptance. We need to learn to love ourselves first, in all our
glory and our imperfections. If we cannot love ourselves, we
cannot fully open to our ability to love others nor our potential to
create. Evolution and all our hopes for a better world rest in the
fearlessness and open-hearted vision of people who embrace life.*

–John Lennon

**All religions, spiritual teachings, and sacred books—at their
core—can be distilled into one word, which is love.** Even the
Old Testament can be distilled into one word—love. For example,
if Adam and Eve had chosen to eat from the "Tree of Love,"
rather than the "Tree of Judgment," they would not have lost the
higher, love-based consciousness necessary for experiencing the
proverbial "Garden of Eden." The Ten Commandments also can
be distilled into the essence of love: if we truly love one another,
we could not kill, steal from, or covet anything belonging to
them. Additionally, the primary law of the Hebrew people is to
"Love the Lord, thy God, with all thy heart, soul, strength, and
mind." Jesus also confirms this in the New Testament and adds:
"Love one another as I have loved you." In so doing, he completes
the message that we are to love all—God, ourselves, and others.
He is also pointing out that we demonstrate our love *for* God by
loving each other.

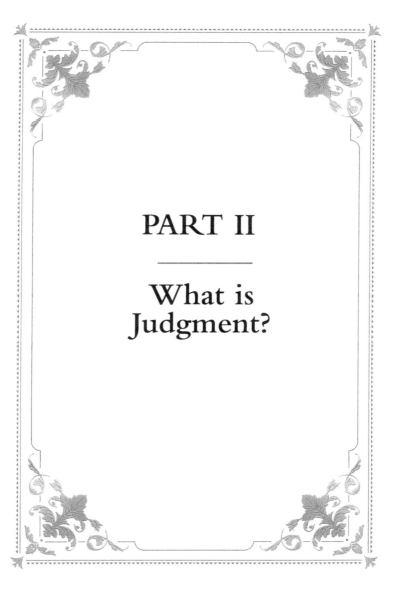

PART II

What is Judgment?

CHAPTER 2

What is Judgment?

If love is all that truly exists, then how and why is it that we so often feel anything but love and so often act any way but lovingly?

It's because ("once upon a time") we forgot who we are, which is love. This, then, led to our acting in unloving ways. **To this day, we reenact this same digression: We are love, but we forget that we are love, and so we begin to act unlovingly—to ourselves and others.**

The good news, however, is that deep down it is impossible to completely forget who we are—Love. The bad news, however, is that we have started believing in our new, false identity and have given it a name—fear. Therefore, **the opposite of love is fear—which is what we feel when love seems to be absent. And what we fear is that we are no longer the presence of love—which is impossible**.

Unfortunately, **as soon as we perceive and judge that we are no longer the presence of love, we are also establishing the belief that we are separate from love**—which also, by default, establishes the false belief that we are separate from God—the Ultimate Source of Love.

However, when we are in our right mind, our loving mind, feeling a sense of oneness is natural. Our true self has no problem feeling oneness with any person or thing that we perceive as love. That's because true love is as safe and attractive as our memory of Heaven, and perfect Oneness. But **we can perceive people and things as being love or loving only if we ourselves are in a state of love**. Otherwise, when we slip into a state of mind wherein we doubt our identity as love, those doubts begin to leak out onto our outer world and its inhabitants. This outer world begins to reflect back to us our own doubts and fears that there is anything but love. So, what we believe inside begins to manifest on the outside. When this happens, the judgments we have against ourselves (that we are no longer the presence of perfect love) create so much anxiety within that we desperately push these judgments and feelings out onto others, in an attempt to "get rid of them." Projecting our inner doubts and fears onto others seemingly gives us a momentary, but false, sense of relief from the self-judgments that have been causing us angst.

If we choose to believe, or judge, that someone or something is flawed, then we believe that person or thing is potentially dangerous and should be avoided or discarded (perpetuating the pattern of separation). Also, such activating of the lower, analytical, judgmental mind (symbolically found in our solar plexus chakra—the home of the ego) keeps us from activating our higher, intuitive, loving mind (symbolically found higher up in our heart chakra—the home of the soul).

Consequently, **letting go of judgment is possibly the most intelligent choice we can make on our spiritual journey**. After all, judgment (as opposed to discernment, which is aware of options and chooses love) is absolutely worthless. **Judgment accomplishes nothing of value because it has no real value**.

Judgment is ultimately made up of inaccurate assessments about what we think, believe, or perceive. And when our mind is in judgment and projection mode, we are incapable of neurologically or spiritually seeing anything accurately.

One underrated means of letting go of our judgments is to consider whether or not the person(s) we are judging committed an unforgiveable "sin" or merely made a mistake. If we can come to accept that what we once referred to as "sins" are more accurately simply mistakes, it immediately shifts the way we perceive the person(s) or event(s) involved. This shift results from the belief that mistakes are forgivable but sins are not. So **if we alter our perception from the person having committed a sin to having made a mistake, we can immediately shift our response from the unforgivable judgment of a sin to the potential forgiveness of a mistake**.

Mistakes are always forgivable
if one has the courage to admit them.

–Bruce Lee

Judgment is made up of two decisions: 1) to perceive someone or something as flawed and 2) to insist on maintaining this perception—consciously or unconsciously.

One way that we experience judgment on a day-to-day level is to formulate an opinion and then do our best to prove that it is right or correct. But the truth is, **as soon as we formulate an opinion, we most likely are already wrong or inaccurate**. Any opinion that perceives a difference between this and that, wherein one is right and the other is wrong, is likely based on judgment or misperception. Seeing through the eyes of love, on the other hand, tends to help us perceive things merely as either love or a cry for love—either one holding the potential to end as love. Forgiveness, therefore, is merely the choice to answer a cry for love *with* love.

We have two different options for releasing judgments: 1) We can choose to nip judgments in the bud *before* committing them—deciding in advance not to judge. 2) We can choose to release judgments *after* we have begun to commit them. Either option allows us to change our minds about judging, which can then lead us into love—our only healthy, peaceful choice.

> *A dream of judgment came into the mind* [of God's Child].
> *And in that dream was Heaven changed to hell, and God made* [into an] *enemy. How can God's Child awaken from the dream? It is a dream of judgment. So must he judge not, and he will awaken.*

> —*A Course in Miracles*

Judgment creates constriction in our lives. Therefore, judgment can produce constriction in our emotions, such as a lack of peace; OR in our finances, such as a lack of funds; OR in our body, such as a lack of health.

We experience what ultimately is the same, original self-judgment over and over again on a daily basis—all too often unconsciously. For example, while on the earth plane, we seem to have sickness, but it is judgment that causes sickness. We seem to have financial issues, but it is judgment that causes financial issues. We seem to have racial issues, but it is judgment that causes racial issues. In fact, **all forms of human longing and suffering are rooted in false beliefs and judgments—**

judgments that can be recognized, released, and replaced with higher beliefs in harmony with the Loving Truth of God. The process of forgiveness helps us to accomplish this transformation and return to Love.

Although thoughts and acts of judgment can seem to scare or anger some people, the only emotion worth feeling, where judgment is concerned is one of sadness. This is because judgment is a sad and unfortunate condition—which deserves love and compassion. This can be seen when we realize that for someone to judge another person, they first have to have judged themselves—which is sad. It also means that whatever judgment they had about themselves seemed so terrible to them that they literally had to project or force those terrible feelings onto someone else in an attempt to be free of them. And that too is very sad.

Most people think that judgments are only the negative things we speak about others. But before we *speak* any words of judgment, we already are feeling the negative *emotions* of judgment. And before we feel the *emotion* of judgment, we already are thinking the *thoughts* of judgment. And **before we think the *thoughts* of judgment, we already are holding a *belief* of judgment.**

So, although it helps us not to cause unnecessary offenses to others—which is good—**repressing our judgmental words, emotions, and thoughts can too often be an act of denial.** The truth is, to eliminate judgment, we have to heal our judgmental beliefs—the beliefs we hold deep in our heart and soul. And since most people do not know how to access their core beliefs in their heart and soul, it becomes clear that we need some help with this process. That's why *true* healing involves prayer and spiritual work.

To heal ourselves of the tendency to cast judgment, it helps to more fully understand the process of judgment. One primary misperception is that our judgment comes after the perceived event we have judged as negative. The truth is, however, that before an event even occurs, we have already set it up according to our preconceptions—the characters, behaviors, and the potential reactions. So, it's senseless to judge others or external events—given that we unconsciously set them up the way we prejudged they would be. Therefore, **self-knowledge, responsibility, and self-forgiveness are needed before we can experience true forgiveness of others**.

One of the most challenging paradoxes about judgment is that **just because we are learning not to judge, it doesn't mean we should pretend something harmful hasn't happened or isn't happening**. And since this appears to be a paradox, the means of dealing with such issues can seem confusing or contradictory—that is, until they are properly translated, or until we remind ourselves that we must learn to **know the truth but respect the illusion**.

Another commonly mistaken view about judgment is that we should "refrain from judgment" in any way. Although this seems like sound advice, it actually is a superficial view. **Attempting to refrain from all judgment can result in denial and dishonesty**. Such refraining from judgment can originate from a sense of duty and obligation, rather than from the authentic understanding, or the evolved consciousness, of a truly forgiving mind. Fortunately, as we evolve spiritually, we develop a deeper understanding of judgment.

For example, in our early stages of spiritual development, we might think of judgment as being those moments when we judge ourselves or others for the way they look or dress or the way they behave. But **as we grow and become more spiritual in our understanding, we come to recognize that our judgments are much deeper than what we think of people on a surface level**. We begin to access the deeper source of our judgments: the belief that we all are flawed in our souls and therefore are not the holy beings that God Itself Created us to be.

Ironically, however, **our very decision to maintain this judgment (that we are unholy) is what mostly creates the evidence that we are indeed flawed—just as we had suspected**. After all, we can't perceive ourselves as being holy or "good" while holding a single judgment against ourselves or others. We can't have any clear perception of reality while holding any judgments—because judgments cloud our perception.

> *Men are disturbed not by things that happen but by their opinion of the things that happened.*
>
> **–Epictetus**

Although we think that we see "rights" and "wrongs" every day; from the viewpoint of ultimate truth, such judgments are impossible. We fail at what we think we see most clearly, simply because whatever input we receive from our eyes or senses automatically stands between us and the truth, or untruth, of what we perceive. In other words, the body and the physical senses portray, or manifest, the illusion of separation. **The only way we can see truth is by choosing to see beyond what we think we see with our eyes and senses and to see with the vision of Christ.**

It is not up to you to change your brother, but merely to accept him as he is. Any attempt you make to correct a brother means that you believe that correction by you is possible, and this can only be the arrogance of the ego. [Instead], *correction is of God . . . He will teach you how to see . . . without condemnation, by learning how to look on everything without it.*

—A Course in Miracles

Despite the appearance of numerous atrocities and hurtful behaviors on our planet, *A Course in Miracles* is adamant that being angry or holding judgments is *never* justified—no matter what seemingly has been done to us or others.

JUDGING OTHERS

No matter how it may seem, **judgment is never merely a perception of something in the present moment or as it truly is now. Instead, judgment is always rooted in the past:** 1) All of our seemingly current judgments are actually rooted in the beginning of time when we originally judged ourselves as flawed and separated from God and thus from each other. 2) Our seemingly current judgments are also simply reactions to opinions, events, and/or programs that we've formulated in an earlier part of our life or in our past lives.

[Love's] *purpose is to suspend judgment entirely. Judgment always rests on the past, for past experience is the basis on which you judge. Judgment becomes impossible without the past.*

—A Course in Miracles

When we judge someone, it's typically either because we perceive them as having something we *don't* have (but want) and that they will not give it to us OR because of something we feel that they have done *to* us or would not do *for* us. In either case, the judgment is related to the theme of someone else having power over us. And since no one actually does have any such power, it's worth considering that we should focus more on forgiving ourselves for ever believing such nonsense, rather than on needing to forgive them.

> *When you correct a brother, you are telling him that he is wrong. He may be making no sense at the time, and it is certain that, if he is speaking from the ego, he will not be making sense. But your task is still to tell him he is right. You do not tell him this verbally, if he is speaking foolishly. He needs correction at another level, because his error is at another level. He is still right, because he is a Son of God. His ego is always wrong, no matter what it says or does.*

> *—A Course in Miracles*

Here, the Course is telling us that **rather than pretending that people are wonderful—even when they are clearly doing something horrible—our job is to remind ourselves that no matter how people behave, in reality they are still Holy Children of God** and deserving of our prayers that they heal their cause for being hurtful.

> *When a brother behaves insanely, you can heal him only by perceiving the sanity in him.*

> *—A Course in Miracles*

Spirit calls to us to surrender our interpretation of the behavior of others to the Holy Spirit to remind ourselves of the Truth of their being. The Course confirms that **whenever people are coming from their ego, they are, in fact, always "wrong"**—because the ego and its behaviors are always **wrong** (and "make no sense"). Yet we are asked that instead of pointing out this fact to them, **we can quietly let the soul of the person know that we are present to affirm their innate goodness**—despite their behaviors.

> *When a brother acts insanely, he is offering you an opportunity to bless him. His need is yours. You need the blessing you can offer him. There is no way for you to have it except by giving it. This is the law of God, and it has no exceptions. What you deny you lack, not because it is lacking, but because you have denied it in another and are therefore not aware of it in yourself. Every response you make is determined by what you think you are, and what you want to be is what you think you are. What you want to be, then, must determine every response you make.*

> *—A Course in Miracles*

The bottom line is that, **if we find ourselves intent on proving others wrong (for coming from their ego), it only confirms that we too are then coming from our ego.** And no resolution is possible between two conflicting egos.

All judgments that relate to the world of form are merely symptoms—the tip of the iceberg. As previously mentioned, the core problem of any judgment is that we have judged others as being less than God created them to be. The root of any judgment, however, is that we have first judged ourselves as being less than God created us to be and then projected that judgment onto others and the world.

There are several ways that the ego keeps us focused on the outer world, and one of the primary tools in its arsenal is the habit of fault-finding. In fact, the ego convinces us that it is somehow beneficial to find fault with everyone whom we love or hate. And the ego uses our lower, analytical mind to find these faults. Just as our analytical, or divisive, mind looks into telescopes and microscopes to zero-in on things "out there" (confirming that we are separate from those things) this same lower mind looks with a scrutinizing eye upon everything to confirm that it is somehow flawed.

Ego-illusions [or perceptions] *are quite specific, although the mind is naturally abstract. Part of the mind becomes concrete, however, when it splits* [or separates]. *The concrete* [lower] *part believes in the ego, because the ego depends on the concrete.*

—A Course in Miracles

Once we allow the inner critic (the ego) to pass judgment on (or attack) us, or others, we are no longer objective, but instead are biased in favor of the ego's thought-system. And, contrary to what we believe we want, **we energetically become a part of the very thing we are judging and end up having to face the karmic results of our judgment**.

Those that find fault with others will find fault in
themselves; for they are writing their own record—
[everyone] *must meet . . .* [deal with] *that which they*
have said about another; for so is the image, the soul of the
Creator in each body, and when ye speak evil of or unkindly
to thy brother, thou hast done it unto thy God.

–Edgar Cayce

JUDGING SELF

**Whenever we judge any-one or any-thing, it is because
we have already determined—in the deepest recesses of
our souls—that we, ourselves, are flawed and incapable of
experiencing the Consciousness of God** and all the gifts that
come with this Consciousness. We then project these judgments
of ourselves onto others.

If you point out the errors [or flaws] *in your brother's ego*
you must be seeing through yours. . . To perceive errors
in anyone, and to react to them as if they were real, is
to make them real for you. [Then] *you will not escape*
paying the price for this . . . because you are following the
wrong guide and will therefore lose your way.

–A Course in Miracles

Although all of our problems stem from the original belief (or
illusion) that we separated from God, it is not this belief that is the
real issue. The real issue is that we judged ourselves for having had
such a belief (thereby helping to make the illusion seem real).

We assumed that merely having the belief (that we were flawed and ended up separate from God) would cause this false belief to manifest. However, this is not possible because none of what we were assuming *is* actually possible. Nevertheless, our belief that we had separated from God caused us to feel afraid, which then made us judge ourselves as guilty for having had the thought of separation. We now experience this same, original self-judgment and its numerous manifestations over and over again on a daily basis.

MOVING BEYOND JUDGMENT

The only valuable judgment is essentially to judge (or come to understand) that judgment is worthless or valueless. In fact, the true meaning of the proverbial "Last Judgment" is that each person, and mankind as a whole, will eventually come to this realization and end all judgment, which also means we will no longer experience the effects of judgment—physically, emotionally, financially, and so on. In other words, **the last judgment marks the moment in time wherein we cease making judgments**, thus making our most previous judgment, our last judgment.

> [Cease judging.] *The ego cannot survive without judgment, and is* [then] *laid aside accordingly.*
>
> *−A Course in Miracles*

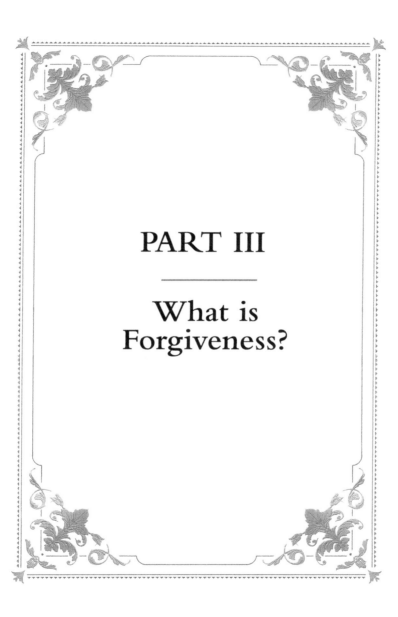

PART III

What is Forgiveness?

CHAPTER 3

What is Forgiveness?

In its purest sense, forgiveness is synonymous with the word "restoration." This is because forgiveness restores our soul to seeing the light and truth of whatever it was that became darkened by judgment or resentment.

What are we forgiving? We are forgiving not only our judgments but also our resentments and painful memories. In actuality, **painful memories have two parts: pain and memories**. As we heal, the pain usually dissipates first. Then, the memories too fade away, but only if we consistently practice forgiveness and refrain from slipping back into judgment. Otherwise, the memories themselves (even without residual pain) will haunt us and keep us in an unhealed state of post-trauma.

One way to define forgiveness is to describe it as three general stages:

1. We begin by forgiving others—which means forgiving our judgments of them.
2. We shift towards forgiving ourselves—which means forgiving our judgments of ourselves.
3. We shift into understanding that there is no value in judging anyone—which means that once we have forgiven others and ourselves, there is no one, and no thing, left *to* forgive.

Although this progression is something that everyone will ultimately come to understand and experience, **it actually can cause more harm than good for us to attempt to jump to a stage of forgiveness that is further along than we are ready to accept**. Also, it is never appropriate for us to try to force others into premature attempts to forgive. For example, it would not be helpful to tell someone who was recently traumatized by another person that what they are perceiving is just an "illusion," and they should, therefore, immediately recognize and accept that there is really nothing to forgive. This is much like telling someone to "get over it!—which is quite insensitive and could cause more hurt.

As long as we are committed to healing at the soul level, **we will progress from one stage of forgiveness to another, but only when we are ready**. There is nothing wrong with postponing a deeper level of practicing forgiveness until we have gained the benefits of utilizing a level of forgiveness in which we presently believe.

In the first stage of beginning to forgive others, we detail, analyze, and judge what others have done to us and attempt to "let it go" and "forgive them."

In the second stage, when we look more deeply at the hurt others have seemingly caused us, we recognize a pattern behind these reoccurring hurts and that healing this pattern (or core cause of the pattern) is our responsibility. The fact that this pattern has not been healed means that we have not yet chosen to heal the core issue. This also, by default, means that we have chosen to remain in an unhealed and unforgiving state of being. For this, we need to forgive ourselves.

Then, in the third and final stage of forgiveness, we recognize that once we release and forgive ourselves and others, there is no one left to either condemn or forgive. We understand that all things we perceive to be either right or wrong, forgiven or unforgiven, are just holographic symptoms reflecting our beliefs that we are separate from God/Love and each other. And since we truly never have separated from God, none of this illusion/dream truly, or actually, took place.

> *To blame others for your misfortunes, shows you are in need of education. To blame yourself, shows your education has begun. To blame no one, shows your education is complete.*
>
> ### –Epictetus

Forgiveness can also be viewed as beginning with these three steps: 1) *Recognize* that we have likely judged someone (including ourselves) as being less than holy and divine. 2) *Accept* that this decision has manifested as an internal or external negative experience due to the choice we made to judge *and* that we can make a different choice—a choice to practice love and forgiveness for everyone involved. 3) *Surrender* the entire experience and the results of our new choice—to forgive—to the spirit of God. In other words, here is where we "let go and let God."

Forgiveness then ends with these two final steps: 4) Refill the space left by whatever we surrendered, with something new—the Holy Presence of God. 5) Give Thanks that we have chosen to make the healthy decision to release the people and memories of the past and replace them with the gifts of God, which leads to a whole new life.

> [Indescribable] *beauty will rise to bless your sight as*
> *you look upon the world with forgiving eyes. For forgiveness*
> *literally transforms vision, and lets you see the real world...*
> *The smallest leaf becomes a thing of wonder, and a*
> *blade of grass a sign of God's perfection.*
>
> ―*A Course in Miracles*

People often assume that in order to be forgiving, we are supposed to love and forgive abusive behaviors. For example, it's often asked, "How are we supposed to love people who abuse children or animals?" The answer is simple, yet profoundly important to understand: **we are *not* asked to love the *abuse* nor the abusive part of that person. We are asked only to love the Christ within that person that they have long forgotten.** In other words, **to forgive someone means to see them as they truly are**, as God created them to be, rather than the form in which they have temporarily shown up.

> *Be mindful. If you see someone causing harm to you or*
> *another, offer him/her advice; and if he apologizes and*
> *changes direction, forgive him/her. Even if he causes harm*
> *against you seven times in a day, but sincerely returns seven*
> *times with an apology and amends, forgive him.*
>
> ―*The Bible*

Forgiveness can manifest in many forms: finding solutions to problems that seemed unsolvable, manifesting more prosperity, improving our relationships, and experiencing improvements in other areas of our lives.

When we realize that it's only our limiting beliefs (resulting from judgments) that cause challenges in our lives and that forgiveness releases all such issues, we will use forgiveness techniques to help manifest everything we need while on earth—"our daily bread."

> *What could you want that forgiveness cannot give? Do you want peace? Forgiveness offers it. Do you want happiness, a quiet mind, a certainty of purpose, and a sense of worth and beauty that transcends the world? Do you want care and safety, and the warmth of sure protection always? Do you want a quietness that cannot be disturbed, a gentleness that never can be hurt, a deep, abiding comfort, and a rest so perfect it can never be upset? All this forgiveness offers you, and more. It sparkles in your eyes as you awake, and gives you joy with which to meet the day. It soothes your forehead while you sleep, and rests upon your eyelids so you see no dreams of fear and evil, malice and attack. And when you wake again, it offers you another day of happiness and peace. All this forgiveness offers you, and more.*
>
> *—A Course in Miracles*

To forgive can involve choosing to be a bridge between any two people or situations that seem unhealed or separate. On a daily basis, however, **forgiveness often takes the form of mediating between two or more thoughts within our own mind** (choosing between our right mind and the ego mind) and their manifestation with other people. So forgiveness is useful in every area of our lives—whether our internal thoughts or their external manifestations.

When we truly forgive, the brain cells that remember harmful things that seem to have been done to us get dismantled or unplugged. Then, new memory cells are created to remind us that beneath all the events in our lives, there was always love—even where we once could not see it.

I will forgive and this will disappear.

—A Course in Miracles

A general guideline to help us discern when we are thinking judgmental thoughts (whether consciously or unconsciously) is to observe how we are feeling— emotionally. If we normally feel peaceful and joyous, it is usually a sign that we are forgiving. If, on the other hand, we most often feel anxious and depressed, it may be a sign that we are being too judgmental—toward ourselves and/or others.

Every time we meet people, whether we like them or dislike them, it is a sacred opportunity to see them beyond our opinions of like or dislike and instead through eyes of holiness. If we choose to maintain our personal opinions/ judgments of people, we are merely reinforcing past judgments and the power of their egos and our own. This, of course, makes no sense because the past is gone and now offers us nothing. So who in their right mind would prefer choosing past judgments? Instead, we have the option of living in the "now," or the present moment, where a holy experience awaits us.

In a holy experience, instead of judging or even perceiving another person as horrid or unforgivable, we become open to seeing the beauty of their soul. And there is no beauty on earth that compares to seeing or feeling that beauty of soul we all, in truth, share. It's even beyond the beauty of a near-death experience, wherein we see an incredible light and feel the love of those dear to us who have passed on. This does not imply that their hurtful egos or behaviors become, or are, beautiful, because they are not. Yet, the soul within all beings is indeed beautiful and reflects the pure Light of Spirit.

Most people interpret forgiveness as being a spiritual or religious concept, practiced by someone who wants to experience a cleansing of old feelings or regrets. In such cases, forgiveness is usually seen as a nice thing to consider but hardly a practicality that affects our day-to-day lives. But the opposite is true. Forgiveness is *so* practical that if people had the courage to truly forgive, it would improve their lives in all areas. Forgiveness can cure disease, improve our relationships and finances, give us creative inspirations, and much more.

Again, forgiveness is a process of restoration with enormous practical benefits. However, **for us to experience the miraculous benefits of forgiveness, we have to be willing to see ourselves and others in a divine light**—or as we all were prior to our belief in separation. Any hesitation to witnessing the beauty within everyone's spirit, by default, limits our ability to experience this beauty within ourselves.

Seeing the divinity of ourselves and all others might seem difficult or even impossible, but that's only because it *is* impossible if we attempt to do it on our own. But that which is impossible for man is always possible for God. Therefore, **it's essential that we call upon the Spirit of God to assist us in seeing people and events as they truly are**, which is the same as seeing as God Sees, rather than seeing through the eyes of the ego that st up our previous programs of judgment and condemnation.

*The real world is attained simply by the
complete forgiveness of the old.*

—A Course in Miracles

The statement found in the Lord's Prayer—"Forgive us our debts as we forgive others"—can be restated as follows:"Forgiven are our debts as we have forgiven others" OR "We are released (forgiven) as we release (forgive) others."This means, in part, that our lives will improve as quickly as our willingness to love and forgive others. However, **if we say, "No," to living a life of love and forgiveness, we keep ourselves bound to the past and unaware of the present moment, wherein Peace is found.** When we say, "Yes," to true forgiveness, we immediately shift into our natural state of "grace"—not grace as a type of spiritual amnesty, but the grace that exists in the mind and soul of one who has accepted his or her original identity—holy and sinless.

Another quality that helps us reach such profound expressions of forgiveness is that of gratitude. *A Course in Miracles* teaches that when we practice true forgiveness, we naturally begin to feel and express a sense of gratitude for even those who seemingly have done the most horrific things.

It's not that we are to feel grateful for people traumatizing us, but we *can* be grateful for what we choose to learn from the experience—which usually means we will not experience it again. For example, we can be grateful that we learned the power and value of forgiveness. We can also be grateful that our seeming "enemy" magnified and reflected to us some of our deepest core issues that were previously unseen. And now, by having these issues exposed and choosing forgiveness, we ourselves have reached a higher level of consciousness—meaning we are now much closer to returning Home. It is for this (not the actual painful human experience) that we are grateful.

*Forgiveness is the fragrance that the violet sheds
on the heel that has crushed it.*

−Mark Twain

In addition to having some mistaken *beliefs* about forgiveness, we also have mistaken (or false) *techniques* for *practicing* forgiveness. These tend to prolong the forgiveness process. Of course **any attempt to forgive is better than none, but there are some methods that are more progressive, authentic, and effective than others**.

These mistaken (or false) forms of forgiveness include forgiving: 1) out of pity or 2) out of obligation or 3) as part of a "deal" or 4) by pretending that we are "past all that." Also, **false forgiveness is usually founded on keeping someone in the assigned role of "victim," which automatically suspends any chance to experience healing and true forgiveness**.

The ego, too, has a plan for forgiveness . . . [a plan that] *makes
no sense and will not work. The ego's plan is to have you
see error clearly first* [allowing a false sense of pride and
righteousness]*, and then overlook it.* [But, by making it
real, you] *cannot overlook* [or forgive] *it.*

−*A Course in Miracles*

The more dramatized the roles of victim/victimizer (or "good guy/bad guy") remain, the more entrenched the hurt will be, thus rendering forgiveness even more difficult. There is no escaping the fact that it is not possible to experience true forgiveness while hiding, denying, defending, or protecting our hurts, or by pretending that we have no hurts because we have "forgiven them all."

No matter how clever, or crafty, we (and our ego) may be, if we retain any judgments, consciously or unconsciously, they will inevitably surface and be seen, spoken, felt, and/or expressed—especially in our relationships and interactions with others. Also, **it will be apparent that we still are holding judgments (even as we claim to want to forgive) when we consistently keep talking about the old wounds and issues**—especially when our words reveal that we have made little or no progress in our desire to forgive.

Nothing is hidden that will not be disclosed, nor is anything secret that will not become known and come to light.

—The Bible

One important thing to remember about *true* forgiveness, however, is that just because we have chosen to work on forgiving an issue (such as an old wound), the full effect of that decision often is not experienced immediately. Instead, we usually experience such effects over a period of time—minutes, days, months, or even years. So **it's wise to know, in faith, that all is well—even when we cannot yet see the manifested results**. Otherwise, we may be tempted to doubt the efficacy of our forgiveness, merely because the past judgments and traumas still seem to cast a shadow into our lives.

Forgivenessss is still, and quietly does nothing.
It merely looks, and waits, and judges not.

−*A Course in Miracles*

If our hearts are filled with anger, hurt, or pain, we will witness and experience lives that reflect these conditions. But **if our hearts are filled with unconditional love, as well as true, authentic love and forgiveness for all that once felt unloving; we will just as certainly witness such reflections in our lives**—usually in the form of Love, Peace, Joy, and Abundance.

Again, there are several levels of forgiveness; but at whichever level we practice, the bottom line is that **if we fail to completely forgive someone or something, we cannot experience the best life possible**. Ultimately, all excuses for not having forgiven are merely subtle forms of unconsciously choosing to retain our belief in separation and therefore our belief that we are undeserving of a better life.

Since it is our choice to see through the eyes of forgiveness, which offers us entrance into Heaven and the holy vision of light within ourselves and others, then it stands to reason that **forgiveness is our only purpose (or function) on earth**. And since judgment is ultimately rooted in our original belief that we are flawed and separate from God, then forgiveness is ultimately rooted in the healing of that belief.

Let us this day accept forgiveness as our only function. . .
Forgiveness is the only function meaningful in time. It is
the means the Holy Spirit uses to translate [judgment and
separation] . . . *into salvation* [love and oneness].

−*A Course in Miracles*

FORGIVING OTHERS

Some of us refuse to believe that we hold any judgments at all about others, and perhaps even claim to feel "only love for everyone." Of course, if this were true, we would probably have ascended by now. However, as long as we notice the difference between the colors of people's skin or perceive a difference between victims and victimizers, our souls retain some untrue perceptions that originate in unhealed judgments. God holds no such judgments or perceptions of differences. Therefore, it is our destiny to also hold *no* judgments *whatsoever.*

*Be kind to one another, tenderhearted, forgiving one another,
as God in Christ forgave you.*

—The Bible

Whether the decision is made consciously or unconsciously, when we choose not to forgive a person or an event that seems to have harmed us, it also means we are then, by default, choosing to be in pain—physically, emotionally, mentally, and/or in our life's circumstances. Furthermore, we will feel guilty for holding this resentment. Then this feeling of guilt will cause even greater pain in our heart and soul.

*So if you are seeking to commune [meditate] with God, and
suddenly remember that your brother has a grievance against
you, cease your attempts at communion. Choose instead to first
bring peace and healing between you and your brother, and then
return to communion.*

—The Bible

The solution to our guilt (and to all challenges) is the miracle of true forgiveness—which necessitates utilizing more authentic forms of forgiveness. Then we can look our judgments in the eye and ask to see others (and ourselves) as God sees them. Then our previously seen judgmental perceptions can shift to holier visions and feelings.

Many human beings believe that forgiveness begins with an act of "pardoning" someone for their hurtful behavior. However, in its ultimate sense, forgiveness begins when we no longer believe that other people's behavior has power over us. Instead, we have come to understand that **only the ego can harm or be harmed. And as we learn to identify with our spirit instead of the ego, the harm (along with the ego) vanishes—as do the ego's memories**.

The ego's interpretation of the Bible saying "Vengeance is mine . . . says the Lord" means that God will punish those who have harmed us far more than we ever could. And although it may seem like good advice because it sounds like it's telling us to trust in God, it ends up making God seem like a Mafia hitman—one in which we trust to "take care of that issue for us." Spirit's interpretation of this biblical saying, on the other hand, is far different. Spirit bids us to entrust all of our anger and hurt to God so that God can help us to dispel it by teaching us to see and understand it differently.

Forgiveness is somewhat like waking up from a nightmare involving other people doing something hurtful to us. When we wake up, we choose not to hold any anger or resentment towards the people who seemingly harmed us in our nightmare. And so we release them for the roles they played in the dream.

*Forgiveness recognizes that what you thought
your brother did to you has not occurred.*

—A Course in Miracles

Of course it seems easier to forgive those whom we have deemed "deserving" of our forgiveness or whom we have had the time to gradually *choose* to forgive. However **the real work of forgiveness comes from those people who catch us off guard when we're not in the "mood" to forgive.** Although these may seem like challenging people with whom to practice healing, these are the folks who offer us an opportunity for some of our greatest advancements. We can learn to laugh at the fact that we were caught unprepared and attempting to ignore a potential for forgiveness, but we still need to follow through with forgiveness. We will then begin to reap the rewards of peace and joy that come from choosing to forgive everyone at all times.

*To give a problem to the Holy Spirit to solve for you means
that you [truly] want it solved. To keep it for yourself to
solve . . . is to decide it should remain unsettled,
unresolved, and lasting in its power.*

—A Course in Miracles

Forgiveness takes courage, persistence, and a willing mind. But it also takes the recognition that forgiveness is a choice. For example, **even if (by human standards) others have indeed harmed us, we can still choose to forgive them and release them (and ourselves) from the prison, or hell, of hurt and**

blame. And, as we release them, we release ourselves. After all, the sole purpose of life on earth is that of healing ourselves and others through the giving and receiving of love, which is best achieved through forgiveness.

> *Fear condemns. Love forgives. Forgiveness thus undoes*
> *what fear has produced, returning the soul-mind to the*
> *awareness of God. For this reason, forgiveness can truly be*
> *called, salvation. It is the means by which* [the illusions of
> harmful behaviors] *disappear.*
>
> *—A Course in Miracles*

"**Forgive them for they know not what they do . . .**" **is a message that Jesus sent from his Divine Self to his human soul**. That's why he said, "Father, forgive them . . ." It was his soul-self telling his human-self to forgive his abusers, for they know not what they do. He would NOT have been the Christ if he had not understood that he was speaking to his own, human self—while also teaching all of us how to see beyond the false witnessing of this world.

FORGIVING SELF

Most people think forgiveness is about releasing others from what they have done to us. In truth, however, forgiveness is not about what *others* have done to us but about what we have done to *ourselves*. **We have chosen to forget our divinity, and we have never completely forgiven ourselves for this decision**.

Human beings typically avoid any true practice of forgiveness. Yet those of us who *do* attempt to engage in such a practice usually do so without realizing that whomever and whatever we are attempting to forgive, mirrors the forgiveness that needs to take place within ourselves. In other words, **as we judge, so are we judged, and as we forgive, so are we forgiven**.

Therefore, to think forgiveness is about letting someone else "off the hook" for taking our money, our partner, our health, or even our life proves we have a limited understanding of forgiveness.

Attempting to forgive others at such a shallow level confirms that we still identify with those events and the pain they caused us. It preserves the illusion that we are victims who feel threatened and attacked. This leads us to defending and attacking back, which usually results in our feeling guilty or having to justify our actions.

If we know who we are in truth and reality, we will clearly understand that nothing of value can be taken from us and that no one can harm our soul, our true self. When we understand the larger, truer picture of life and know that it is impossible for our true self to be harmed, forgiveness becomes unnecessary. Therefore, **instead of focusing on forgiving others, we eventually progress to forgiving ourselves for forgetting our true identity (which led to our feeling of being vulnerable to the harm of others)**.

As we develop a deeper understanding and thus practice a truer and more authentic form of love and forgiveness, it is essential (until all fear and illusion are gone) that we don't buy into our projected fear that made them seem to attack us (or us them). Instead, we choose to know and see the truth of our true identity and the true identity of others. This provides our healing, and "As we heal, we are not healed alone."

MOVING BEYOND FORGIVENESS

Most mystics and Masters believe that everything in this universe of space/time is an illusion. However, there is one great paradox: **there is one illusion, forgiveness, that was created by God as the solution to all other illusions. In other words, forgiveness is the reflection or manifestation of God's love on the earth plane**.

> *God does not forgive because* [God] *has never condemned . . .*
> *Yet forgiveness is . . . the reflection of God's Love on Earth.*
>
> *—A Course in Miracles*

Forgiveness is part of the illusion of this world because, like this world, it too is temporary and will one day cease to exist, because it will no longer be necessary. And since, as the saying goes, "life is but a dream," **forgiveness is unique in that it is the only dream that depicts humanity as waking up from the dream** (making it similar to a "lucid dream").

Another way of saying this is that the absolute necessity for forgiveness in *this* world is not a necessity in Heaven. Therefore, **as hard as it may be for some to believe, forgiveness itself is ultimately an illusion**. But, forgiveness is the *only* illusion created by God and was created to undo all *other* illusions.

Although we clearly dislike our ego's image that others are mirroring back to us, we just as easily could choose to let them mirror our spiritual self, which then would result in our deepest gratitude for the light we see in them. **If we choose to see love and light in others, we rise with them in oneness to Heaven.** But why wait? Whenever a person or event seems to attack or challenge us, we can, in the present, deal with it by responding as though we are already in Heaven—which obviously evokes a response of forgiveness. If, on the other hand, we choose to see the flaws and darkness in others, we "fall," alone into hell—the hell of our own making.

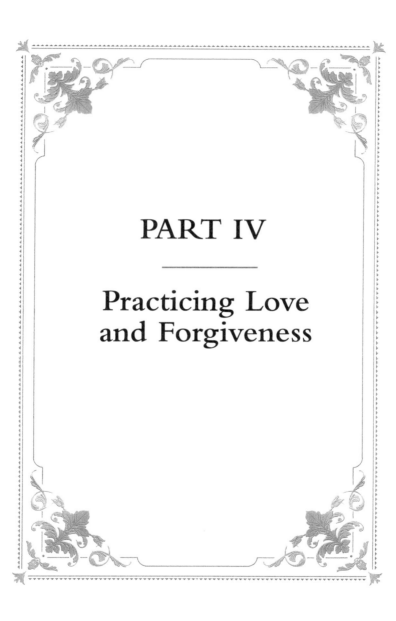

PART IV

Practicing Love
and Forgiveness

CHAPTER 4

An Introduction to Exercises in Forgiveness

The following two chapters feature beginning and advanced exercises for practicing forgiveness. There are three important points to keep in mind while moving forward into these chapters.

The first important point is that no matter what technique(s) we prefer or find most valuable, all human beings on earth should practice at least one exercise in forgiveness of themselves or someone else, *every* day of their life.

The second important point is that the so-called "beginning" techniques are part of a necessary foundation in our understanding of forgiveness. For example, "Forgiveness Technique #1" is so perfect in its simplicity and effectiveness that if we were able to practice effectively only this *one* technique, we would need no other.

The third important point is that even though these exercises are labeled "beginning" and "advanced," it does not imply they are for "beginners" or "advanced" students of spirituality or of forgiveness. Quite the contrary, such labeling of students on the path as "beginning" or "advanced" (which can lead to judgment) is counter-productive to the goal and purpose of these exercises.

While it is true that the advanced techniques are more "progressed" than the beginning techniques, the main thing that sets them apart is this: the **advanced forgiveness techniques require us to take a higher level of responsibility**. And although this might sound easy, often it isn't. In fact, **taking greater responsibility includes recognizing that once we feel complete with forgiving others, we are ready to shift/ progress into forgiving ourselves**. This is primarily when it's time to move into the advanced techniques.

In the meantime, it is helpful to remember that **every attempt to forgive is at least an attempt to move in the right direction**. Initially, the best some of us may do is to apply forgiveness in the form of simply trying to forget that something happened or someone did something to us—while affirming the old adage that "time heals." This is clearly neither an effective nor a deep way to practice forgiveness, but it's at least a valid start.

Then we might try praying for the power to forgive someone, while still insisting that the other person is a "bad guy" (victimizer) and we are a "good guy" (victim). This form of forgiveness leaves a lot to be desired, but again, it's a move in the right direction. Next, we might sincerely believe that we are finally forgiving other people because we have decided to rise above it and "overlook their wrongdoing." Once again, this falls short of true and lasting forgiveness.

Another fairly common form of forgiveness is the use of rationalizing, wherein we say things like: "Well, I'm beyond all that and have come to accept that the traumas and events of my past made me who I am today. I would not be who I am without those experiences. So I am grateful for all of it and have forgiven it all." And although our need to sometimes rationalize things is understandable, this is just a form of denial and is a potentially dangerous affirmation. **We never should affirm that "we would not be who we are without our traumas and abuses."** This suggests and affirms that we actually need such experiences to become a person of value, and that simply is not true. If we survived difficult events and were able to move forward, it does not mean we need to credit our abuse or our abuser. We need only be grateful that we made some good choices that helped us to get through it all. And **even though we survived, it doesn't mean we have learned to truly thrive—which is what comes when we reach the highest level of forgiveness**.

Next, we might grow to a level of consciousness wherein we finally begin to apply a more sincere and effective form of forgiveness—nearly the highest form of forgiveness—*compassion*. At this level of consciousness, we begin to understand that **the harms people do to others come from a painful place within themselves, and so what they need is healing, through love and compassion**. However, despite the high level of consciousness it takes to practice compassion, this level of forgiveness still affirms that the hurtful actions of others are *real* but can be dissolved with enough love.

Although these limited forms of forgiveness (where we still believe that someone actually has caused us harm) are not the ultimate expressions of forgiveness, it certainly wouldn't be right to shame (or judge) anyone (including ourselves) for practicing forgiveness only at this level. Instead, we might introduce them to the concept of a higher level of forgiveness, but without rushing them to practice a higher level they do not yet understand.

Lastly, we reach the highest form of forgiveness: "Spiritual Forgiveness," which is the practice of seeing and understanding that there is nothing to forgive. **When we are upset by something someone has done, forgiveness—in its truest sense—elevates consciousness to a level that affirms whatever we thought happened actually *did* not (and *could* not) occur.**

Since God (Our True Self) is a unified, pure state of Consciousness, It sees only purity and innocence—never seeing flaws and therefore seeing nothing that needs to be forgiven. Consequently, **at this level (the highest of human understanding), we realize that there is ultimately no-body and no-thing to forgive.**

Spiritual forgiveness, which is true forgiveness, provides a release from every disturbance and anxiety that comes from feeling abused or traumatized. And although such emotions are relatively understandable and acceptable in this world, when we recognize our divinity and that no one has the ability to harm us, such emotions will not occur because their cause will not be perceived or experienced.

This level of forgiveness is beyond "forgiveness through compassion," since **seeing as God sees tends to make "errors" more laughable (and absurd) than forgivable.**

At this point, there is no longer an "us" attempting to forgive. Instead, we simply forgive, as God Guides us to forgive. In other words, we choose to see all things as God sees them, and, in so doing, it becomes impossible for us to see anything as bad, wrong, negative, or in need of forgiveness. In other words, **the** ultimate practice of forgiveness is to realize there is nothing to forgive, and all that we once thought needed forgiveness was merely an illusion—a bad dream of angst, resulting from our false beliefs related to separation.

Experiencing this level of true forgiveness is not the same as being in Heaven Itself, because in Heaven there is nothing left to forgive. However, true forgiveness is similar enough to Heaven to make it nearly impossible to tell them apart because they both are free of judgment and leave us with an incredible feeling of love, peace, and joy.

> *Can you imagine how beautiful those you forgive will look to you? Nothing you see* [on earth] *comes near to such. Nothing . . . has ever brought you even a little part of the happiness this sight will bring you. For you will . . . behold the beauty the Holy Spirit loves to look upon.*

—A Course in Miracles

Again, forgiveness might start with a focus on others, but it shifts towards a focus on ourselves, and eventually concludes when there is no one left to forgive.

CHAPTER 5

A Beginner's Guide
to Forgiveness

Although some people might assume that they are ready for advanced techniques of forgiveness, it's wise (and a statement of humility) to first study some of the more basic techniques.

One reason for this is that **our ability to forgive is, to a large extent, contingent upon our awareness and understanding of the *essence* of forgiveness**. It's also contingent upon how ready and willing we are to release judgments about what are sometimes significant people and/or life-altering events. And since these people and events may sometimes have had significant effects on our lives, we are not always ready to release them. Therefore, **if we try to fast-forward into the more advanced techniques of forgiveness, it could place too much pressure on our mind and our nervous system**. Furthermore, if we are not ready to forgive at a more advanced level, such attempts could also prove to lack authenticity and therefore might fail, thus causing us to feel ashamed and inadequate. In other words, such attempts could cause more harm than good, which is a clear sign that they were not the right choice.

This does not mean that by beginning with the more basic techniques we will never shift towards the more advanced techniques. On the contrary, **it is always possible that shifting from one level of forgiveness to another is only days, or even hours, away**.

Also, **even if we believe we are ready to utilize the more** *advanced* **techniques of forgiveness, it would be foolish to ignore the** *basic* **techniques, as these are sometimes the better ones to use**—especially for certain given situations.

Ultimately, what is the main difference between basic and advanced techniques of forgiveness? It clearly isn't that the basic techniques are somehow less effective. Instead, the main difference is that the basic techniques are usually simpler and primarily focused on forgiving *others*. The more advanced techniques, however, usually are more detailed and are primarily focused on forgiving *ourselves*.

BASIC FORGIVENESS TECHNIQUES

So where do we begin? It's wise and healthy to begin our practice (hopefully a daily practice) with those who first come to mind when we think about the people and events that we perceive as having most negatively affected our lives.

And remember, **forgiveness is more of a process than a single event. Therefore, we often experience forgiveness in stages**—which is why people may think they've forgiven someone, only to find later that they have to deal with more unhealed pain. So let's do our part to forgive, while being careful not to become impatient. The results are definitely taking place, of that you can be certain. Sometimes these results are profoundly obvious. Other times they are as subtle as a single leaf falling from a tree.

Basic Forgiveness Technique #1
REFUSE, CHOOSE, AND BE WILLING

This first technique is possibly just as valuable, in its own way, as the most advanced technique of forgiveness. It is profoundly simple, as well as profoundly effective, and involves the following three steps:

1. **Refuse to hate**—means that no matter what anyone has done to us, we must refuse to hate them. Insisting on hating them actually keeps us hooked to them and guarantees that we block all hope of experiencing the Peace and Joy of God that comes from forgiveness.

2. **Choose to learn**—means that we are open to learning any and all things/lessons that we can learn from our previously limiting or traumatizing events.

3. **Be willing to love**—means that we are affirming that no matter how a person has behaved, there is a spark of God's Light deep within them—albeit often invisible to us. And although we are asked to be willing to love that spark of light, we are certainly not asked to put ourselves in harm's way by remaining in any unhealthy environments that are not congruent with love.

Basic Forgiveness Technique #2
EVERY DAY AND NIGHT

Here is a forgiveness technique that applies to all people in the world and should be put into practice each and every day. As a form of spiritual house-cleaning, make it a practice to extend some form of forgiveness (including any of the techniques in this book) to every person (or event) entering your mind.

1. If, at any time, day or night, a person (from the past or present) pops into your mind—even if it seems arbitrary—consider that the Spirit of God might very well be bringing that person into your mind to remind you that some extra healing or release needs to be shared.

2. Then, notice the person whose image arises and repeat to yourself: "I recognize that the image of this person is arising and that it likely means there is something not yet completely forgiven between us. (This is important to say even if you are intellectually convinced that there is nothing left there to forgive.)

3. Next, silently say to yourself: "I now choose to give this person to you, God, with a knowing that they deserve Your love and blessing. And by giving them to You with an intention of their highest good, I too will receive this same love and blessing."

4. Give thanks that this is so, AND soak in the gratitude from the soul of the person you had in mind, who appreciates what you have done for yourself and for him (or her). The person may not be consciously aware of their gratitude for your prayer; however, their soul is aware, and that is all that matters.

Basic Forgiveness Technique #3
SOUL-LEVEL HEALING PROCESS (Short Form)

This is the short form of the Soul-Level Healing Process. [For more details about the longer form of this process, see my book: *Healing the Heart & Soul*.] This forgiveness technique is usually experienced as a deep and powerful healing process. Here it has been simplified into a five-part prayer. When repeated sincerely from the heart, it has deep and profound effects.

Repeat the following either quietly to yourself or out loud:

1. **Recognize**: "I Recognize I am struggling with _____ (insert the issue of your concern)." This issue might be an illness, a challenge in a relationship, the inability to buy a new house, the loss of a job, etc.
2. **Accept**: "I Accept that hidden behind this situation are my unhealed wounds and lessons (known and/or unknown)."
3. **Surrender**: "I Surrender to God both the problem and my unhealed wounds that I know lie beneath the surface of what I think I see."
4. **Refill**: "I Refill all the space (left by the issues I just surrendered) with all that God truly intends for me, including Love, Peace, Joy, and Abundance."
5. **Give Thanks**: "I Give Thanks that this process is complete and is already bringing me miracles of healing. Thank you! Thank you! Thank you! And so it is!"

Basic Forgiveness Technique #4
FROM *A COURSE IN MIRACLES*

Here is one of the simplest and most beautiful exercises for forgiveness found in *A Course in Miracles*. Although it ends with an awareness of forgiving ourselves, the beauty of its description of forgiving others is worth including it in this section of "Basic Forgiveness Techniques," which involves forgiving others.

1. Begin this longer practice period by thinking of someone you do not like, who seems to irritate you, or to cause regret in you if you should meet him; one you actively despise or merely try to overlook.

2. Now close your eyes and picture him in your mind, and look at him for a while.

3. Try to imagine some light in him somewhere, a little gleam that you had never noticed. Try to find some little spark of brightness shining through the ugly picture that you hold of him.

4. Look at this picture until you see a light somewhere within it, and then let this light expand until it covers him, making the picture of him appear beautiful and good.

5. Look at this changed perception for a while, and then return your mind to the one you formerly disliked and can now see as safe and can call a friend.

6. Perceive him now as more than friend to you, for in that light his holiness shows you your savior, saved and saving, healed and whole.

7. Let him now offer back to *you* the light you see in him, and let your new friend [spiritual brother/sister] unite in blessing you with what you gave. Now are you one with him, and he with you.

8. Now have you been forgiven by yourself.

Basic Forgiveness Technique #5
FROM *A COURSE IN MIRACLES*

Here is another forgiveness exercise found in *A Course in Miracles*. Once again, the wording is beautiful—almost poetic.

1. Begin the longer practice periods by repeating, "God is the Love in which I forgive."

2. Close your eyes and spend a minute or two in searching your mind for those whom you have not forgiven. It does not

matter "how much" you have not forgiven them. You have forgiven them entirely or not at all.

3. If you are doing the exercises well, you should have no difficulty in finding a number of people you have not forgiven. It is a safe rule that anyone you do not like is a suitable subject.

4. Mention each one by name, and say: "God is the Love in which I forgive you" [insert name].

5. After you have applied the idea to all those who have come to mind, tell yourself: "God is the Love in which I forgive myself."

6. The exercise should end with a repetition as originally stated, "God is the Love in which I forgive."

NOTE: Another way to use this technique is to apply it at any time during the day when you become aware of any kind of negative reaction to anyone, present or not. In that event, tell him (or her) silently, "God is the Love in which I forgive you."

CHAPTER 6

An Advanced Guide
to Forgiveness

It is best not to proceed into this chapter until you understand and have practiced the essentials of the previous chapter—the beginner's guide to forgiveness. However, if you do feel that you are ready, it's important to know that **you *can* try these techniques—even if you do not totally understand their principles**.

For many people, understanding and accepting the advanced stages of forgiveness might seem somewhat overwhelming. That's because the **advanced concepts of forgiveness require faith in a way of thinking and feeling that is foreign to most of us**. It also requires taking responsibility and a willingness to accept that we might have been seeing people and the world in a way that was simply inaccurate.

If we see the Christ Light in others, we are automatically seeing the manifestation of our choice to forgive and see through holy eyes that can see only love and innocence. On the other hand, if we see flaws in others, we automatically are perceiving our own judgments, which then condemn us to the karmic results of such judgment. So, whatever the view of others we happen to see, it confirms how we have chosen to perceive them—innocent or flawed.

When we see flaws in other people (things we dislike), a part of us believes that had they only behaved differently, we would have seen them differently. But in truth, we perceive in them the judgments we had already assigned to them (even if we have never met or seen them before). In other words, **we already have negative judgments of ourselves—which we then project onto other people in an attempt to rid ourselves of our own conscious or unconscious feelings of guilt and self-loathing**. Of course, this means we owe them an apology (as, in truth, we owe ourselves) for our own projected negative self-judgments. For this reason, the ancient Hawaiian prayer (*Ho'oponopono*) encourages us to pray to all others: "I'm sorry. Please forgive me. I love you. Thank you!"

Again, anything we perceive that others have done to us (good or ill) first has been "assigned" to them by us to manifest either our projected self-love or self-loathing. And we will know which self-perception they are reflecting back to us by the way we feel about their presence, words, and actions.

Furthermore, even though **it may look and feel as though others have clearly "caused" our hurts and wounds, the truth is, others are more often merely "rubbing up" against our pre-existing wounds.** By releasing all negative perceptions of self and others, however, our soul is restored to its original state of grace. All problems (from health to financial) are related to our wounded mis-perceptions and are healed (sometimes instantaneously) through the miracle of forgiveness—by choosing love over fear, or reality over illusion.

*The real world is attained simply by the
complete forgiveness of the old.*

—A Course in Miracles

Practicing Spiritual Forgiveness at this level is based upon the understanding that since God, or Love, is all that really exists; anything else must be an illusion. So, **whenever we see an error in another, we are not seeing as God sees, which means we are not seeing the Truth about ourselves and someone else**. And, since we are not seeing with the eyes of God and are not seeing the Truth, then what we are seeing is false. Therefore, to react as though it were true would be insane, since we would be reacting to something that is not really there or is not really happening. Thus, **once we understand that anything we've ever experienced that seemed to lack Love must have been false—an illusion—it becomes easier to accept that there is nothing to forgive.**

If it is a struggle to believe that in the final stage of forgiveness there is nothing to forgive, it may be helpful to recognize that since God is Love and Love can do no harm, then **God can neither *cause* nor *experience* trauma**. And if our True Self is One with God, then our True Self has neither *caused* nor *experienced* any trauma that needs forgiving. Therefore, **the more we surrender to our True Self (rather than identify with our limited, ego-based self), the more our seeming traumas disappear**. Then, rather than needing to practice forgiveness, we realize that there is nothing to forgive—and we find the "peace that surpasses understanding."

Spiritual forgiveness heals us of the misperception of separation from God and from each other—which is an important part of our return Home. Spiritual forgiveness enhances the process of experiencing miracles in every aspect of our lives. Therefore, **when we truly forgive, we are coming closer to "being as God," because to truly forgive is to see and feel only the light within ourselves and others**, which is to see as God sees.

Forgiveness is the healing of the perception of separation.

—A Course in Miracles

When we truly ask for the strength and clarity to forgive at the highest level, we no longer are asking for the strength to forgive someone who has upset us. Instead, we are asking for our mind to be healed of our perceptions, or judgments. **When truly forgiving, we are not denying that something seemed to have occurred within the illusion/dream, rather we are asking for release from our interpretation (judgment) of the event.** This includes the release from the power we allowed our negative perceptions, or judgments, to have over us—judgments that affect the quality of our daily lives.

Therefore, forgiveness is a process that takes practice, determination, tenacity, and willingness to perceive things anew. Forgiveness also requires humility because it means admitting that everything we once held against ourselves and/or others was a mistaken illusion.

Forgive and you will see this differently.

—A Course in Miracles

Although we begin our practice of forgiveness with those whom we perceive as needing to be forgiven, **when we move into advanced stages of practicing forgiveness, we eventually discover that we actually need to forgive everyone on earth and beyond—as projections of our own false belief in separation**—which ultimately is forgiving our self for having had this false belief.

TAKING RESPONSIBILTY

Although the preliminary or basic techniques for forgiveness might still address "others" as being the problem and the focus of our forgiveness, **advanced forms of forgiveness require sincere soul-searching in order to take greater responsibility for our part in whatever may have occurred**.

At first, **the idea of our playing a part in the manifestation of the events in our lives that were not pleasant and empowering may sound confusing and even cruel or insensitive.** But, that's only when we view it from our ego's perspective, rather than with our soul's vision.

When practicing forgiveness, **we are called to take responsibility for any part we may have played—even if unknown to us consciously—in contributing to the harms done to us**. Again, this may seem almost impossible for human beings (who see everything in this world as either black or white with no gray area) to understand. With such a viewpoint, we are either victims or victimizers. If we are not the ones causing harm, then we must have been the ones receiving harm and were therefore, the helpless victims. There is no gray area.

That's why true forgiveness—advanced forgiveness—takes courage and responsibility. **We must be willing to face the ultimate reality that nothing ever happens by chance.** When someone harms us, we must be able to accept that on some level we were open to it. Yet we might say, "Who, in their right mind would want to think that they were 'open' to experiencing any form of trauma? Something must clearly be wrong with this picture!"

For this reason, many people are not open to the concept of advanced healing. It seems as though advanced healing is asking us to acknowledge that in some manner we "caused our own traumas and abuses"—even if the traumas and abuses occurred when we were children. And although this might be an accurate description of advanced forgiveness at the level of human ego-perception, it's not an accurate description at the level of the soul's vision where true forgiveness and healing take place.

When viewing things from a limited human perception, it would be accurate to say that we rarely, if ever, cause our own traumas and abuses. However, deep inside, within the soul (or unconscious self), there is much more going on than we can imagine. Here, deep within our psyche, we hold unconscious lessons and agendas, karmic debts, as well as the patterns of our unhealed wounds and core beliefs. All of these have the ability to attract to us any number of manifested forms of trauma.

On the outside surface, the traumas seem unrelated to anything else. On the inside depth of the psyche, however, all these things are connected. But **most people are not aware of these connections (our part in attracting life's traumas) until they either experience soul-level healing OR they die and pass over onto the "other side," wherein it all becomes much clearer**. Of course, when the latter option takes place, it's too late. Then we must return to earth again to discover these connections and try to heal/forgive them.

MIRRORING

Most of us on the spiritual path have heard of the term "mirroring." But many people understand only its shallow connotation. For example, you may have been expressing a frustration about someone in your life, and a friend exclaims: "Well, that person must be mirroring something about yourself that you don't want to look at!" Although your friend may have meant well, such use of the term and concept of "mirroring" is limited and over-simplified.

The concept, or "law," of mirroring basically can be explained as follows: **The world (and universe) around us can be viewed as a three-dimensional, holographic manifestation of the conscious and subconscious thoughts within our minds and souls. Therefore, it can be said that the universe is reflecting (or mirroring) back to us whatever we are feeling, thinking, and believing consciously and subconsciously.** In other words, the *external* world that we perceive is merely mirroring the *internal* world of our beliefs, thoughts, and feelings. These outer reflections are meant to capture our attention and to show us something about our inner selves that we probably are ignoring and need to see magnified and projected literally onto the people and world around us.

> *You must look in before you look out*
> *. . . As you decide so will you see.*
>
> **—*A Course in Miracles***

What most people fail to understand is that these outer reflections can be either positive or negative. In either case, though, **our job is to recognize our projections and bring them back into ourselves, so we can "own" them and learn what they are trying to teach us**.

When these projections onto others are mirroring (or reflecting) *positive* messages or traits of ourselves (as with persons whom we admire or find attractive); they either reveal traits that we ourselves have, but are denying, OR reveal traits we need to nurture, but thus far are failing to do so.

Conversely, **when our projections are mirroring (or reflecting) negative messages, issues, or traits of ourselves onto others (as with persons who irritate or repulse us), they show us issues that we may either dislike and/or are trying to ignore in ourselves.** By projecting these issues onto people and conditions in the outer world, our souls are prompting our human selves to take notice and eventually recognize their own unhealed wounds (triggered by these traits) that are in need of forgiveness and release.

In the case of *negative* mirroring, **often it is our most intimate relationships that most assist us in healing by mirroring (or revealing) our deepest fears, judgments, doubts, and insecurities.** Although we may be able to ignore or hide from these issues while living alone, when we choose to interact closely with others (as in an intimate relationship); it is nearly impossible to ignore our hidden issues. However, we rarely will jump at the chance to recognize the opportunity before us.

It truly takes courage and vulnerability to recognize and accept that if someone is upsetting us, **it is not only what the other person is saying or doing (or failing to say or do) that is causing an issue. It is the other person's mirroring and triggering of an unhealed wound existing within us that is causing (or contributing to) our feeling upset.** Ironically, we probably would remain unaware of the issues lurking in the deep recesses of our souls or subconscious selves were it not for the people who mirror these negative traits to us.

Besides having two *versions* of mirroring—positive and negative—mirroring also takes one of two *forms*: literal and symbolic. It is easier for most people to see the *literal* form of mirroring: where something outside of us manifests as a literal reflection of our thoughts or beliefs. For example, manifesting a controlling person in our life may mirror that we, ourselves, are actually (at some level) a controlling person and that we need to heal or observe this tendency. *Symbolic* mirroring, on the other hand, rarely reflects anything of literal (or "face" value) significance. In such a case, we may have a controlling person in our lives, but it is clear that we are in no way a controlling person ourselves. So, why then, are we manifesting a controlling person, and what could he or she be reflecting to us? We have to look within ourselves to discern the symbolic meaning.

For example, when we ask ourselves what "controlling" people symbolize (or mean) to us, we may find that they denote either insecurity in us or a possible fear of authority (control). It could be then, that it is either this insecurity (need for the security that control may offer) or the fear of authority that needs healing, rather than a literal tendency to be controlling of others or situations.

In the context of forgiveness, **one of the most important things about the concept of mirroring is that we come to accept that if the universal law of mirroring ("As within, so without") truly exists, then we also have to consider that ALL events on the outside (including traumatic events) are there to mirror what is on the inside of us, individually and collectively, consciously or unconsciously**. Since all outside events may be mirroring either love or fear, unity or separation, we *likely* have something we can learn from all experiences and eventually bring those of fear and separation to closure through forgiveness.

ADVANCED FORGIVENESS TECHNIQUES

Even though the particular issue to be healed/forgiven differs with each person, the following techniques are diverse, powerful, simple, and very effective for all issues. Any exercises that involve repeating something to yourself can be made easier if someone reads it to you or if you record your own voice taking you through the steps (which may need you to pause the recording at times to allow for processing). These forgiveness techniques also can be used by you when guiding others through the forgiveness process. All techniques that involve the healing or altering of consciousness require the extra time for preparing a private space and beginning with some centering breaths.

Advanced Forgiveness Technique #1
HO'OPONOPONO

The following is an example of a forgiveness technique that originated with the ancient Lemurians and was later passed down as an ancient Hawaiian tradition.

This forgiveness process is known as *Ho'oponopono*, which means "to make right" the wrongs done in our relations. This incredible process not only offers a simple and effective means of forgiveness but, when understood at a deeply spiritual level, also teaches us to take responsibility for whatever we perceive— even if it involves seeing a sick person. However, in the mind of the average thinker, what we see outside of ourselves has little or nothing to do with us, supposedly proven by the fact that it appears "outside" of us.

In *Ho'oponopono*, as well as in *A Course in Miracles*, one of the primary reasons we need to ask others for forgiveness is that we have done them an injustice when we projected our own issues onto them.

The words in this process of asking for forgiveness are very simple and only involve repeating (with heartfelt sincerity and deep awareness) a few short sentences. This can be done silently to oneself when addressed to someone who is ailing or not present. Or, these words can be spoken aloud when making amends to someone present—provided the person agrees to listen. The words of *Ho'oponopono* are as follows:

I'm sorry.
Please forgive me.
I love you.
Thank you!

When combining the words of *Ho'oponopono* with the teachings of *A Course in Miracles*, we also can use the following longer prayer:

Ho'oponopono: "I'm sorry."

ACIM: I am sorry for forgetting your true identity and judging you as being capable of being sick (poor, depressed, etc.).

Ho'oponopono: "Please forgive me."

ACIM: Please forgive me for having projected my unhealed wounds and limiting beliefs onto you, thus co-creating your challenge. I also forgive myself, for I too have suffered by allowing you to bear the cross of my issues.

Ho'oponopono: "I love you."

ACIM: I love you because of who you truly are—God's perfect and holy Child—the Christ.

Ho'oponopono: "Thank you."

ACIM: Thank you for mirroring to me that which needed to be Recognized, Accepted, Surrendered, and Refilled with the

Presence of Truth (the Truth of who we are). As we now stand forgiven (by each other), we also stand healed and one in God, as God. And so it is!

Advanced Forgiveness Technique #2
FROM *A COURSE IN MIRACLES*

The actual process of forgiveness is always taken to a higher level when we understand the primary principles. These principles are summed up in *A Course in Miracles* as steps to achieve forgiveness and are listed as follows:

1. **Identify our negative reaction to a person or event and its true source.** This first step consists of realizing that the cause of our suffering, in any form, is not in the external world, but rather originates within our own minds—being dreamt up by us—like obsessing on a negative thing (that we are flawed) and then manifesting our "punishment." So whatever we seem to experience on the outside has been projected there by our dreaming mind. The first step, then, in forgiveness and healing is that of shifting our focus from illusionary external details of our dream to their origin in our soul-mind, prior to its seeming projection onto an external world.

2. **Make a conscious choice to release this reaction/ interpretation.** Once we have returned the power of causation to our soul-mind, the real issues (our core issues) can be examined and a different choice made. Now that the cause of our angst has been restored to the mind, we are given another chance to choose between the two guides—God's Voice or the ego's voice. This is what *A Course in Miracles* means by "choose again." We are now returned to the place

(our soul-mind) where we made the original decision to believe our ego's counsel, which was to judge ourselves as flawed and then to project our flaws and painful feelings onto others. Whereas before we had chosen to believe the ego's opinion that we are flawed and deserving of suffering, we now can choose to hear a different voice: the Voice of God that tells us we are holy, innocent, loving, and loved. Instead of choosing the illusion of separation, guilt, and shame—which results in judgment and projection—we choose forgiveness and the Reality of our Oneness with God and each other.

3. **Replace the previous feelings and perceptions with the better choices of love, grace, and forgiveness.** By choosing to awaken from the ego's dream of guilt and shame, our eyes and ears slowly open to the Vision and Voice of God. And now, the memory of God's Love begins to dawn within our minds. This remembrance of God is the downfall of the ego's world, for in the presence of God's Perfect Love, nothing remains of a separate self. "Perfect love casts out fear." This miracle of true forgiveness is a shift in perception whereby what always has been true is recognized by those who knew it not, or had forgotten that truth. What has always been is now accepted as our only reality; and the images and memories of fear, guilt, and limitation are no more. This third step in forgiveness is not really a step at all. It's the natural and inevitable result of our acceptance of the first two steps. That is why the Course tells us that the first two steps are our responsibility but that the third step is not. This third step is our return to Love, our return to a state of God's Presence—the moment wherein God reaches down, picks us up, and brings us Home.

Advanced Forgiveness Technique #3
GOODBYE TO OLD SELF

The purpose of the "Goodbye Exercise" varies from person to person. Sometimes it's for saying goodbye to old habits or addictions. It can even be tailored for saying goodbye to others. But it works very well when saying goodbye to an old image of ourselves. This ceremony should be heartfelt and not necessarily repeated verbatim.

1. Begin by creating a private space where you can do this exercise without any interruptions. Then take a minute for several relaxing deep breaths, repeating to yourself, "I am," on the inhale and "Relaxed," on the exhale.

2. Now visualize an image of yourself at whatever age addressed (e.g., the age you were when you experienced a trauma or the age when you adopted certain negative beliefs about yourself). This could be an image of how you looked at any time in your life—child or adult. Then repeat the following:

3. "I am calling you _____ (Insert your name at that time.) into this room, so I can share my feelings about our life and relationship."

4. "My relationship with, and memories of, you have affected my life. They have affected my _____ (Insert whatever areas of your life you feel have been affected, such as health, tension level, nervous system, finances, confidence, relationships, parenting, etc.)."

5. "There were things that happened to you back then, such as _____ (Insert the various traumas or events that affected your life.)."

6. "I learned to see you as _____ (Insert whatever fits, but be spontaneous and do not censor

anything.). Sometimes it is difficult to remember the truth about how we learned to see ourselves negatively, but we might say something like: "I learned to see you as weak" or "unattractive" or "unlovable."

7. "But it's time to let go of my image of you, which means letting you go—unconditionally. This does NOT mean that I am rejecting you or abandoning you. But I have to take my image of you, to a whole new level today, because I did not learn to see you as healthy and happy."

8. Repeat the word "Goodbye" a few times, with about five seconds between each repetition. Then repeat: "With you go all vows, debts, karma, agreements, and contracts between us."

9. Next, visualize the image of yourself reaching up to the top of its (the image's) head and begin to unzip its body. Let the image of yourself unzip the body slowly from the top of the head, down the front of the body, to the navel.

10. Then visualize the image of yourself peeling the body off from the head, then over the shoulders, and down the hips and legs, until at last, the image of yourself can step out of the body and allow it to be dissolved into the earth. As the image of yourself peels off the body, however, visualize a bright body of light being exposed.

11. Take a good look at the being of light who was concealed beneath the previously limited image of yourself. Look carefully and notice how this body of light is not solid, but rather, is made up of sparkles of light.

12. Then, take a few relaxing, deep breaths and draw those sparkles of light into your heart-center—leaving none of the sparkles outside.

13. Begin experiencing how good it feels to become aware of the beautiful being now resting in your heart-center, and

place a hand or two over your heart–center to connect with that energy and/or feeling.

14. Now repeat: "It's great to connect with this part of myself (the being of light). This is a part of myself that cannot be harmed or die or be sick or be flawed in any way. This light is the part of me that is made in God's Perfect Image. And this part of myself is also me, which means I am this light. It's so great to connect with this part of myself. And what God has now brought together, nothing can ever pull apart. I give thanks for this experience and choose from now on to honor this part of myself. And so it is!"

CHAPTER 7

Summary & Conclusion

The world and, in fact, the entire Universe was not made by the physical "hand of God" but by **Pure Consciousness**. God's Holy and *Unlimited* Consciousness Created a *Love-based* Universe called Heaven. Mankind also used consciousness to make a universe, but humans used their *limited* consciousness and fabricated a *fear-based* universe of limitation and separation.

God's Universe is still and calm, creating a sense of Peace and Oneness. Mankind's universe is expanding, creating a sense of distance and separation.

When we think of creating "Heaven on earth," we are unconsciously thinking in terms of "hijacking" Heaven and making it simply an improved version of earth—where everything goes our way. In actuality, however, **we have to let go of our perceptions of earth, as we know it, and allow earth to become Heaven—not the other way around**. This, of course, would cause the disappearance of the material Universe, which can be an intimidating concept. But it is intimidating only to our ego-based self and not to our spirit-based self.

To achieve the state of mind necessary for universal transformation of the Universe would require the surrendering of all judgments we have ever had—particularly the ones that caused us to seemingly separate from Heaven in the first place. These include the judgments that we (or anyone else) are somehow capable of being other than as God Created us.

This ultimate shift in consciousness is not a single future event for which we must be preparing; it is presently a part of each and every issue, small or large, that we experience on a daily basis. In other words, **our shift in consciousness is not coming soon; it is already here**.

From our human perspective, through the choice to forgive ourselves and others, we are pulling up anchor and setting sail into a whole new reality of Peace and Oneness— back to God.

> *The way to God is through forgiveness here. There is no other way . . . God is our Goal. Forgiveness is the means by which our souls return to God—at last.*

—*A Course in Miracles*

AMEN!

Other Books by Grail Press

Healing the
Heart & Soul

Michael Mirdad
$15.00

The Heart of
*A Course In
Miracles*

Michael Mirdad
$20.00

You're Not Going
Crazy...You're Just
Waking Up!

Michael Mirdad
$15.00

An Introduction
to Tantra and
Sacred Sexuality

Michael Mirdad
$15.00

The Seven
Initiations on the
Spiritual Path

Michael Mirdad
$15.00

Creating
Fulfilling
Relationships

Michael Mirdad
$15.00

The Book of Love
and Forgiveness

Michael Mirdad
$15.00

Mother Mary
and the Undoing
Process

Robin Rose
$15.00

To order any of our books or request more information on any of
these publications, please call our office **(360) 671-8349** or visit
www.MichaelMirdad.com for a complete list of books, CDs, and DVDs.

5-DAY INTENSIVES
with **Michael Mirdad**

 **MASTERY & HEALING**

This intensive is great for anyone who is ready to discover new levels of direction, responsibility, balance, wholeness, and a life of fulfillment, as well as learning how to bring God and all spiritual learning into their daily lives and activities. It teaches how to experience the best life possible in every aspect of living. No other single event offers so much! Topics include **physical mastery**–manifesting prosperity, living healthy through yoga and diet, and training in several healing arts; **emotional mastery**–developing psychic abilities, creating fulfilling relationships, and learning advanced emotional healing techniques; **mental mastery**–developing greater focus, learning effective meditation, and discovering your soul's purpose; and **spiritual mastery**–developing a life plan, learning true forgiveness, awakening higher levels of consciousness, and opening your heart center.

 **AWAKENING CHRIST CONSCIOUSNESS**

This intensive is for students and teachers of Christ Consciousness. It teaches attendees to connect with their True (Christ) Self and deeper levels of spiritual awareness. It covers advanced teachings and spiritual concepts, as well as profound levels of application. This program includes initiations into Christ Consciousness through rarely understood mystery teachings of Jesus–some of which were transferred to Mary Magdalene, clearing of various energy centers (chakras), the secret teachings of Christ, Jesus' missing years amongst the Essenes and the Mystery Temples, and experiencing your own spiritual baptism.

ABOUT THE AUTHOR

Michael Mirdad is a world-renowned spiritual teacher, healer, and author. He has worked as an intuitive healer and counselor for over 35 years and is the author of the best-selling books *Healing the Heart & Soul, Creating Fulfilling Relationships, The Heart of A Course in Miracles,* and *You're Not Going Crazy...You're Just Waking Up!* Michael has facilitated thousands of classes, lectures, and workshops throughout the world on Spiritual Mastery, Spirituality, Relationships, and Healing and is commonly referred to as a "teacher's teacher" and a "healer's healer." He has been featured as a keynote speaker in the world's largest expos and conferences and has been on radio, television, and various internet and tele-summit programs. His work has been published in several leading magazines, including *Sedona Journal, Conscious Life Journal,* and *Yoga Journal,* as well as being the cover feature several times in *Evolve* magazine. Michael Mirdad is respected as one of the finest and most diverse healers of our time and is well-known for his ability to share the deepest spiritual teachings in a clear, applicable manner. For more information visit his website: MichaelMirdad.com or go to his public facebook page: https://www.facebook.com/michaelmirdadteacher/.